Discover
Military Equipment
by Amanda Trane

© 2018 by Amanda Trane
ISBN: 978-1-53240-2678
eISBN: 978-1-53240-2685
Images licensed from Fotolia.com
All rights reserved.
No portion of this book may be reproduced
without express permission of the publisher.
First Edition
Published in the United States by
Xist Publishing
www.xistpublishing.com
PO Box 61593 Irvine, CA 92602

When people go to the war, they need military equipment. For thousands of years, soldiers have carried knives. These are throwing knives. They are balanced to spin. Most knives are not balanced to throw at a target.

This is a model of a cannon, a piece of military equipment that has been used for over 800 years. People loaded gunpowder and metal into the cannon, lit the gunpowder, and watched the metal fly long distances.

5

When most people think about military equipment, they think about guns. Revolvers changed warfare in the American Civil War. Both sides had men who used these guns which could be loaded once and then could shoot 6 bullets at a time.

Guns keep changing warfare. Machine guns that can shoot many bullets from one pull of the trigger made it easier for soldiers to defend areas in World War I.

10

This is a grenade. The first hand bombs were used over 1,000 years ago and sometimes exploded before they were thrown. Modern grenades need people to pull the pin and then throw the grenade.

Airplanes changed warfare. Planes were first used during World War I, but they were very important in World War II. This Supermarine Spitfire helped the British fight World War II.

13

This is a gas mask. Many people needed gas masks to fight in World War I because both sides used poison gas against each other. In 1925, the Geneva Gas Protocol was passed which made it illegal for any country to use gas in war.

The radio changed warfare. This radio from World War II made it possible for people to know what their commanding officers wanted them to know.

This is a Tank. Tanks have been used since World War I to move over rough ground.

It has tracks instead of wheels and thick armor to protect the people riding inside.

Submarines changed warfare. The first submarine victory was in 1864, but submarines became popular in World War II.

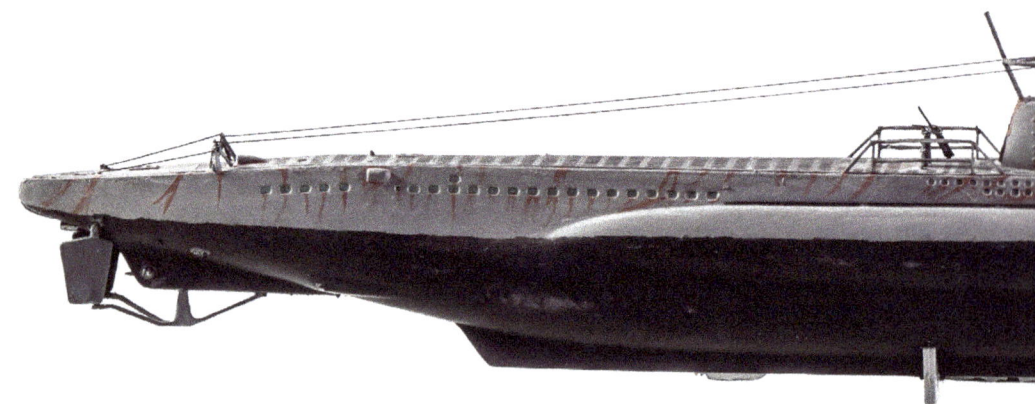

This is a German U-Boat.

22

This is a Nuclear Submarine. Nuclear Submarines use nuclear power to stay underwater for a long time. Sailors usually stay underwater for less than three months, but many submarines can stay underwater for much longer than that.

Helicopters were first used in World War II, but became very important during the Vietnam war.

Helicopters can land in places that airplanes cannot and can move troops to battle or injured people to hospitals.

GPS or Global Positioning System changed warfare. Before satellites people had to count on maps and a compass to figure out where they were. This compass has a metal case to protect it during war.

Recently, Smart Bombs have changed warfare. These bombs can be directed with lasers or satellites to hit a target.

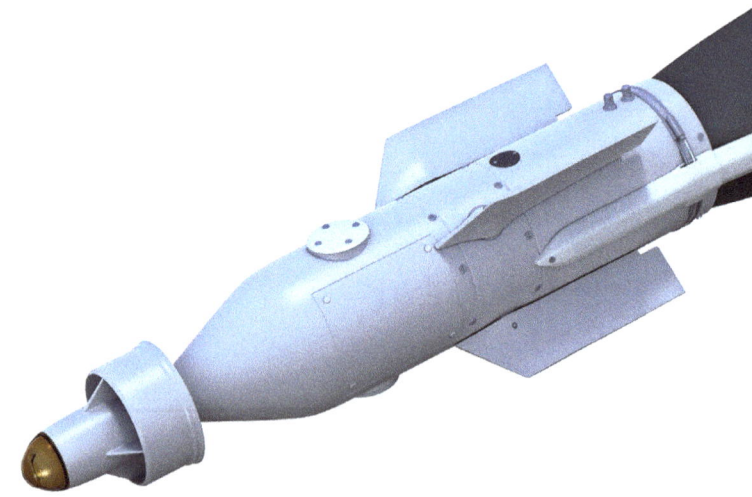

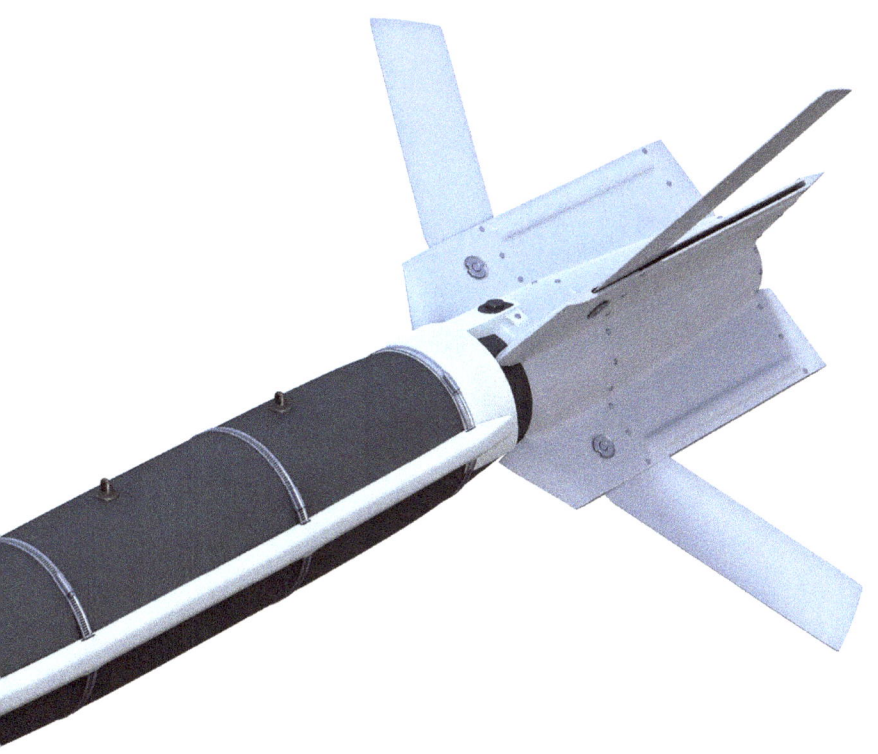

Sometimes, advances in military equipment spread beyond warfare. Next time you see a Jeep, you can think about how this piece of military equipment was first made for World War II, and is now a fun car for anyone to drive.

www.ingramcontent.com/pod-product-compliance
Lightning Source LLC
LaVergne TN
LVHW010317070426
835507LV00026B/3440